OLIVE gets a tummy ache

This book and all those in the Oh, Olive! series are dedicated to our angel baby, Jameson Ryan Koon.

Olive Gets a Tummy Ache: Book 1 of the Oh, Olive! Series
Copyright 2026 by Amy Myers-Koon | amyerskoon@outlook.com
Illustrated by Nastya Bankulova | instagram.com/a_bankulova

Published by Argyle Fox Publishing | argylefoxpublishing.com
ISBN 979-8-89124-101-5 (Paperback)
ISBN 979-8-89124-196-1 (Hardcover)

My name is Olive, and I love food.

I do lots of tricks to get yummy treats from my humans, but sometimes I find treats on my own.

One day, Mom put a gate up in the kitchen. "We have to go to work," Dad said, petting my head. "Be a good girl, and you'll get a big treat when we get home."

Mom gave one last look around the kitchen. "There's nothing on the counter," she told Dad, "so nothing for Olive to get into."

She was wrong.

BREAD

As soon as Mom and Dad walked
out the front door, I spotted a bag
of candy on the bar stool.

I pulled the candy
down, sniffed the bag,
then ate every piece.

Bored, I looked around the kitchen for something else to eat.

A bag of cotton candy was on top of the refrigerator. Mom loves cotton candy, and so do I. It's just one more thing we have in common.

BREAD

I pushed the bar stool across the kitchen floor, then jumped onto it. It was hard keeping my balance, but I did it. Dad would be so proud.

Soon, I knocked the cotton
candy on the floor and ate it all.
Yummy!

I sighed. There was no more candy in sight. So, I laid down against the gate. When I did, I heard a clicking sound. The gate popped open!

In the dining room, I found a
box of cocoa and marshmallows.
Yummy!

I took a big lick and then—
Ouch! My tummy hurt.

When Mom and Dad
got home, I still felt bad.

Mom leaned down and scratched my head. "What's wrong, girl?" she asked.

Dad pointed at the empty candy wrappers. "That's what's wrong."

"Oh, Olive," Mom said.

Mom and
Dad took me
to the doctor to
get medicine.

It took a couple days to feel better,
but I learned my lesson much faster: Too
many sweet treats are not a good thing.

From now on, I'll only eat a
couple at a time, when Mom
and Dad give them to me.